Southern Lady

GRACIOUS SPACES

Southern Lady
GRACIOUS SPACES

{ CREATING THE PERFECT SANCTUARY IN EVERY ROOM }

PHYLLIS HOFFMAN

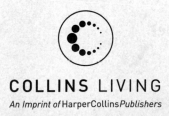

COLLINS LIVING
An Imprint of HarperCollins *Publishers*

Author: Phyllis Hoffman
Editor: Stacey Norwood
Creative Director: Mac Jamieson
Style Director: Yukie McLean
Contributing Stylist: Adrienne Alldredge
Photographers: Marcy Black, Kimberly Finkel Davis,
Sarah Dunlap, Kellie Sliwa
Art Director: Breanne Jackson
Illustrator: Marie Barber
Copy Editor: Anne Garry
Contributing Copy Editor: Nancy Ogburn
Test Kitchen Coordinator: Janice Ritter
Test Kitchen Director: Rebecca Treadwell Touliatos
Food Editors: Aimee Bishop, Loren Wood, Chantel Lambeth,
Virginia Hornbuckle
Digital Imaging Specialist: Clark Densmore
Color Technicians: Delisa McDaniel, Chris Waits
Production Director: Greg Baugh

HarperCollins books may be purchased for educational, business, or sales promotional use. For information please write: Special Markets Department, HarperCollins Publishers Inc., 10 East 53rd Street, New York, NY 10022.

FIRST EDITION

Hoffman, Phyllis.
Southern lady: Gracious spaces : Creating the perfect sanctuary in every room / Phyllis Hoffman. — 1st ed. p. cm.
1. Interior decoration—Southern States. 2. Entertaining—Southern States. I. Title. II. Title: Gracious spaces. III. Title: Creating the perfect sanctuary in every room.

NK2006.H64 2009
747.0975—dc22

2008045814

ISBN 978-0-06-134809-9

09 10 11 12 13 RRD 10 9 8 7 6 5 4 3 2 1

{ DEDICATION }

"Gracious Spaces" is dedicated to my parents, Inez and Oliver Norton, who have celebrated their 80th birthdays at the time of this writing. I have shared 55 years of your lives with great happiness as your daughter.

"Gracious Spaces" to me is any place that has meaning and is filled with treasures from your life. When I was a little girl, you instilled in me that beautiful surroundings can be created with very little. Life wasn't about what you had, but what you did with it.

To Dad, who indulged Mom and me when we dismantled and redecorated a room every time you were away on business. You came home to some big surprises! Your love of woodworking is your hobby that I admire the most. You can take the worst looking piece of furniture and turn it into a beauty with your touch. I especially love the table that I bought when I was a teenager. You showed me how to refinish and together that table took on a new life and new meaning. You look for the beauty in everything and always find it. I love you, Dad.

To Mom, who challenged me to always try new things. You know no limits of creativity. I will always remember the hours we spent making things, sewing, painting, and cooking. Your talents amaze me. It was fun to come home from school and see what you had done that day. You can turn ordinary into wonderful with your special touch. I love you Mom.

Thank you both for loving me, teaching me, and challenging me to be the best I could be. You make each day an adventure. As I was working on this book, I realized that I grew up in gracious spaces where people are the important possessions, and fun is the order of the day. Most importantly, every space in our home was filled with love. And love is the best gift you have given me.

{ CONTENTS }

{ THE SOUTHERN LADY AT HOME }
Bringing Beauty to Unexpected Places

If you open the page to my editor's letter in every issue of *Southern Lady* magazine and look to the right of my signature, you will find one of my favorite verses from Proverbs: "Who can find a virtuous woman? for her price is far above rubies."

The verse is from Proverbs 31, a chapter that paints a picture of the kind of woman I have always strived to be. Like the virtuous woman of Proverbs 31, I have always sought to use my hands, my heart, and my spirit to shape my home and my family, and to do so with a measure of hospitality. When I set out to create the concept of "Gracious Spaces," I turned to these words once more for inspiration and guidance.

As a publisher, I have followed a similar path, and I have been truly blessed. I am surrounded each day by other Proverbs 31 women—both my staff members and our wonderful readers—who feel that beauty is not a vain pursuit, but rather an ordained feminine rite.

She layeth her hands to the spindle, and her hands hold the distaff. She stretcheth out her hand to the poor; yea, she reacheth forth her hands to the needy. She is not afraid of the snow for her household; for all her household are clothed with scarlet.

—PROVERBS 31:19-21

If you believe, as I do, that your home should be a refuge where you can find rest and solitude, then start there when it comes to developing a sense of personal style. Begin with what you love. I have many passions—from playing the piano to creating and collecting intricate needlework samplers. Visitors in my home quickly discern these things about me because every room, every corner, every nook and cranny tell a story about me.

I urge you to try the same approach, and to look at each room not as a place with four walls, a floor, and a ceiling, but rather as a canvas for your heart and soul. Constantly seek and find new sources of inspiration; accrue not only things but ideas and memories.

In my own home, I love being surrounded by treasures that have been given to me by special people, as well as keepsakes from my travels. Collections make a central decorating theme. You can build a room around one item! That is the essence of creating a gracious space—gilding with love, not with things.

That's what we will explore together in the pages of this book—the blessing of gracious living and the fruits of its beautiful labors! We will learn to tap into the deepest sources of our inspiration—from use of color to collectibles to clever ways to showcase these items throughout your home.

BLUE AND WHITE

I was a teenager when I purchased my first set of blue and white china. I saw it in an antique store and put it on layaway, then scrimped and saved and paid it off by the teacup. I still own that set, along with many other pieces and patterns. Blue and white is a theme that lives in my imagination and that frequently takes shape in my home and in my work.

If you love something, wallpaper your life with it, and share your enthusiasm by envisioning new and inventive ways to display and use it. My blue and white pieces—which range broadly by pattern, style, and era—are never tucked away in china cabinets or pantries. They are well worn, oft used, and much loved.

HOSPITABLE TOUCHES

English writer Max Beerbohm once said, "When hospitality becomes an art, it loses its very soul." I have always loved that quote and found truth in it. Graciousness should never be contrived; it should be sincere. And, just as importantly, it should be generous.

Opening our homes to others is a pleasure, and an opportunity to make another feel comforted and cared for. Sharing your most beloved trinkets and treasures with guests will make them feel doubly pampered, especially when it comes to the little touches.

A morning breakfast tray in my home, for instance, would not include only a bite to eat and something to drink, but also my most prized collectibles—perhaps a one-of-a-kind vase filled with flowers, a vintage sterling silver teapot, antique linens, and mix-and-match bone china.

FORM & FUNCTION

As with most families, the kitchen is the heart and center of my home. But from a design perspective, it can be a challenging space to address. Function is key, but form cannot be discounted.

There was a time when kitchens were more utilitarian "service centers" set up chiefly for food preparation and storage. Today, our kitchens are more in step with our lifestyles, and family life tends to gravitate around the kitchen, from pancakes in the morning with the husband and kids to midnight pantry raids with visiting relatives. And we want them to be as pretty as

they are functional. In my own kitchen, a creamy color scheme lightens and brightens, while pieces from my blue and white collections give life to the room. I also like to always keep seasonal fresh flowers in the kitchen; they are beautiful and fragrant, and add a note of cheer.

An airy open-plan layout with an island center that faces an adjacent seating area provides an attractive but dedicated work space, without being a barrier to conversation.

My guests can lounge in leisure as I put the polishing touches on a mix-in-a-minute coffee cake, a dinner for four, or my deliciously calorie-laden strawberry cake. And don't worry—I'll share the recipe in a later chapter!

{ DREAMY DESIGNSCAPES }

There seems to be within all of us an innate yearning to be lifted momentarily out of our own lives into the realm of charm and make-believe.

—DOROTHY DRAPER, INTERIOR DESIGNER

Every woman has a signature style—even if she doesn't know it. Consider the legendary Dorothy Draper. One of my favorite designers, her maverick approach brought her enormous success. A woman whose work embodied the philosophy that "more is more," she was branded bold by her fans and brash by her critics. An audacious use of color and a hurdy-gurdy mix of patterns, textures, and overscale accents marked the so-called "Draper Touch." I have always admired her fearless approach, which she described as "if it feels right, it is right."

Not every woman is born a skilled interior designer; I'm certainly not. But I am a woman who, like Dorothy Draper, loves the idea of finding charm and whimsy in the everyday, then putting my own personal spin on it. You can do that, too. In "Dreamy Designscapes," we will explore some basic concepts: the importance of lighting; crafting an evocative color palette for indoor and outdoor spaces; and, most important, taking a closer look at the unexpected sources of inspiration that are all around us.

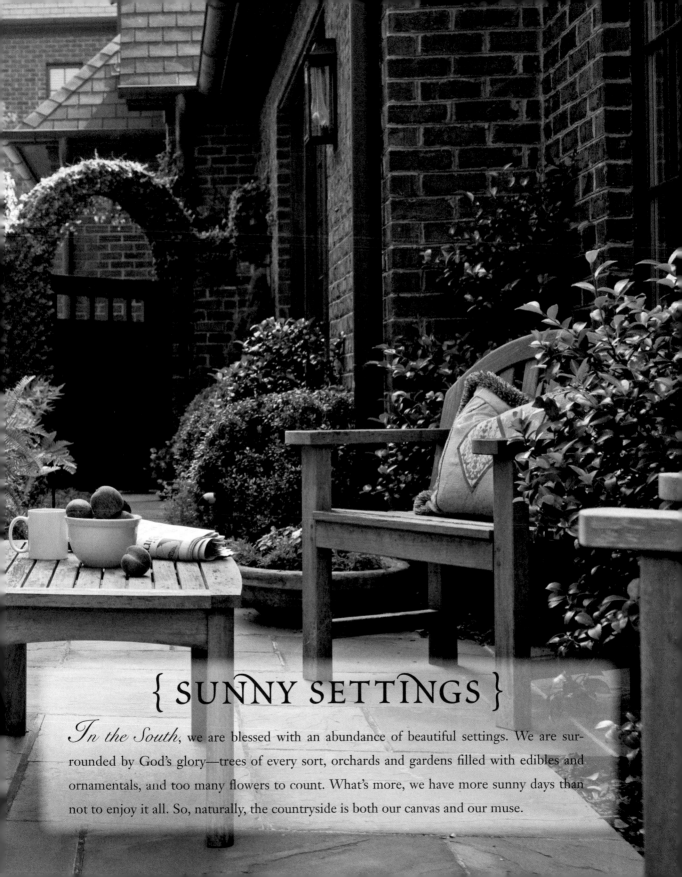

{ SUNNY SETTINGS }

In the South, we are blessed with an abundance of beautiful settings. We are surrounded by God's glory—trees of every sort, orchards and gardens filled with edibles and ornamentals, and too many flowers to count. What's more, we have more sunny days than not to enjoy it all. So, naturally, the countryside is both our canvas and our muse.

OUTDOOR OASIS

Not so long ago, I enjoyed the pleasure of a private tour of Monticello, the mountaintop home of our third president. Architecture, botany, and landscaping were among Thomas Jefferson's numerous pursuits, and he designed the Virginia plantation himself in 1784. These facts I knew.

What I did not know until seeing his work for myself, however, was Jefferson's ingenious technique of bringing the outdoors in and the indoors out. He was fascinated by the idea of maintaining a constant view of the heavens; there are a dozen skylights throughout Monticello, as well as a domed chamber fitted with an oculus that Jefferson referred to as his "sky-room." A true student of nature, he also created several outdoor "rooms."

Designing an outdoor oasis of your own begins with deciding how you want the space to be used. That means choosing the perfect spot.

FOLLOW THE SUN

I am convinced that an outdoor space should be fashioned first and foremost with the position of the sun and stars in mind. Again, Thomas Jefferson's estate is the spark behind this notion.

If you have visited Monticello, you know that the founding father slept directly beneath a skylight so he could ponder the moon and rise with the sun. Also, as visitors almost always note, the main house has no "front." Instead, Jefferson designed an "east front," where the sun rises, and a "west front," from whence it sets.

Like Jefferson, I follow the sun; I love soft morning light just before sunrise and the shimmering glow of sunset. If you are a morning person, too, outfit an eastern-facing spot with comfortable seating and a few accessories. If sunset is more appealing, try a western view, while perhaps adding an umbrella for a bit of shade. And once evening sets in, these pretty perches are equally ideal for a little stargazing.

OUTDOOR SPLENDOR

Southerners love no other time of year so well as spring and summer, when the outdoors beckons so keenly for our company. The phrase "outdoor room" has gained more cachet in recent years, and, as the words imply, the idea is to turn a natural space into a defined living and lounging area.

Though walls are not necessary, some type of overhead protection from the whims of Mother Nature is suggested. Choose comfortable, all-weather furnishings that suit the scale and style of the space. If your "room" is situated with a view of a classic English-style garden, for instance, oversize or contemporary furnishings might clash.

If beds of rainbow-hued zinnias or soft hyacinths abound nearby, try complementary and contrasting shades—the more the better.

Layer color with a base tone, and enrich the look with patterned pillows, candles, odds and ends, and potted plants and flowers. Adding unexpected extras, such as framed prints hung as though indoors, or bone china casually arranged on a wrought-iron table, sets the mood in a playful way.

Also, don't underestimate the impact of lighting in an outdoor room. Subtly placed lighting (I've seen outdoor chandeliers that are to die for) will make the space feel like a lavish escape. Candles and pretty lanterns add glow; outdoor sconces can also be installed. You are making a haven to enjoy day and night for occasions great and small—don't lose sight of that!

FRONT-PORCH APPEAL

The front porch is one of the prettiest and most welcoming parts of a home, so invest in its appearance and comfort. Whether a dramatically furnished veranda or a cozy screened retreat with a view of the neighborhood, your porch should serve as a spot for solace and also as an invitation to visitors.

Front-porch furnishings can be eclectic, but find a cohesive theme—perhaps a unifying color scheme, or furniture from a single school of style or period. Arrange seating areas into smaller and larger groupings to accommodate a multitude of uses for the space, from an early-morning breakfast for two to a comfy spot for opening mail or reading a book.

Accessorize with flowers and plants, both potted and hanging, as well as with a hodgepodge of knickknacks that suit your tastes. Because I know the weather and elements eventually will wear on my most favorite front-porch finds, I bargain shop for such pieces at flea markets, vintage stores, and jumble sales.

SUNNY SETTINGS

The morning sun warms me, especially in winter. A sunroom, ideally located in the eastern wing of a house to catch the morning light, has the feel of a front porch with the conveniences and comforts of an indoor living space.

Minimize or eschew fussy window treatments, relying instead on oversize windows to open up and enliven the room. Though furnishings may be elegant, keep them casually so. Rattan pieces, pillow-strewn settees, and low lighting are perfect for a sunroom, as are airy ferns and other flora. Plants love a sunroom, so year-round beauties will grow and bloom.

Pieces that reflect nature, such as sturdy garden urns or botanical prints, are also lovely, as well as mood-setting. Though color schemes are certainly optional, those that mimic the outdoors can be particularly relaxing and inviting.

{ EXPRESSIONS IN COLOR }

As a child, one of my favorite playthings was a box of Crayola Crayons. The colorful names and the rainbow of hues they represented captivated me: Burnt Sienna, Cornflower, Raw Umber, and Cadet Blue. Like the endless array of options in that iconic cardboard box, color possibilities for the home are equally plentiful and, with the right approach, can be just as playful.

CHOOSING A PALETTE

When I think of the power of color, I am reminded of a beautiful quote by the late writer John Greenleaf Whittier: "Beauty seen is never lost; God's colors all are fast."

I believe you should surround yourself with colors you love! If you're like me, there are countless hues that appeal, each in its own unique way, and each invoking a distinct emotional reaction. White calms and soothes me, but add a tickle of cobalt blue, and I am excited, inspired! On the other end of the spectrum, however, I also adore stand-alone primary shades, and use them throughout my home, indoors and out. I am particularly drawn to fiery, emphatic red. In fact, one of my favorite escapes, my music room, is painted a sunny yellow but accented in an impetuous shade of red. I love the complementary colorplay of the two hues, and both work well with the other primary colors used throughout my home.

When choosing your own color palette or scheme, there are many questions to consider. How will the room be used, and how much time will you spend there? What are the existing elements you are working with—the furniture, accent pieces, and lighting? All of these things play a role in choosing a color scheme.

And, above all, remember one of my favorite golden rules of thumb: Do unto color as you would have it do unto you. If you love a hue, use it plentifully in the gracious spaces of your home. It will inspire you anew each and every day.

BREAK THE RULES

Although I certainly believe that it's just fine to throw "rules" out with the dishwater sometimes, there are occasions when adhering to convention is a beautiful thing.

When choosing a color palette, remember the "60-30-10" design rule: 60 percent dominant shade, 30 percent secondary complementary shade, and 10 percent accent color.

An interior decorator would tell you that typically translates to building the color palette around the walls, followed by major furnishings, and then filling in with touches of accent color. That's a "rule" I'm willing to ignore.

An intimate space is one defined by its character and mood, not its four walls. So look for what moves you, and build around that. Allow that piece or idea to dominate the color scheme, then find other hues, either within the same family of colors or contrasting shades that make the primary color visually pop.

YOUR PERSONAL STAMP

Color is one of the most evocative tools in any creative spirit's arsenal; that is especially true with home decor. Not only does color evoke mood, but it also helps to establish visual boundaries within a room and stamps the space with personal style. When a person enters your home, the colors and design schemes you have chosen speak volumes about you, so choose wisely—a personal inventory might help you make the right selections.

Are you fashion savvy? If the answer is yes, harness that love and use it to create a sanctuary in your home. Colors, like everything else, tend to come and go with the fashion of the day. Remember the shade of seafoam green that saturated the seventies or the hot neon hues that defined the eighties? You might not necessarily want to paint an entire room in those colors, but the subtle use of trendy shades—such as violet and green—is a wonderful way to freshen a room. This works particularly well with accent furnishings, such as window treatments, throw rugs, and smaller pieces.

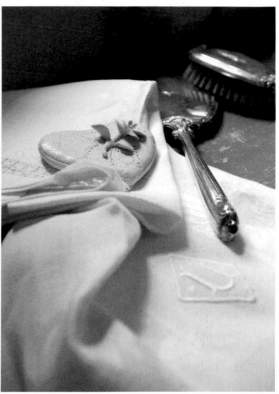

HISTORICALLY ACCURATE

Perhaps you, like me, are a student and lover of history. Look in my home, and you will find the richly pigmented colors of Colonial America not only in my collection of needlework samplers, but also on the color of my walls. These days, you can find numerous interior (and exterior) paint palettes based on specific periods: Federal, Victorian, Queen Anne, Edwardian, Greek Revival, Italianate, Bungalow, and many other options, each reflecting the authentic style and color choices of the era.

Look to the architectural and design details in your home—door casings, moldings, etc.— and choose colors that echo the historic style of these motifs. This helps achieve a soothing visual cohesion and a sense of flow from room to room. Weave those shades in with your own personality and the style of your choosing, whether it's farmhouse chic or Old-World European, and to create a home that's comforting to you and welcoming to your guests.

MOTHER NATURE'S PALETTE

Another way to put together a color scheme is simply to open the nearest door or window and let your eyes take in all that lies before you. Perhaps there is a hydrangea bush blooming nearby. Have you ever seen such gorgeous colors? Periwinkle, whimsical lilac, soft magenta, blushing pink, and gentle ecru—all in one breathtaking flower just begging to be admired and mimicked in a front-porch resting spot, or even more subtly in a handcrafted piece of needlework.

There are literally scores of colors—some estimate as many as 16 million—and you will find most of them in nature, from the greenest pasture to the bluest patch of sky to the sunniest lemon on the tree. When settling on a color scheme for all your gracious spaces, glorious Mother Nature is the perfect guide, and we never tire of her parade of options.

{ SOURCES OF INSPIRATION }

What inspires me? A perfumey peach rose in bloom, delicate blue and white, antique linens edged with the ivory patina of time, the tenderness I feel cradling my newborn grandson as he sleeps fast in my arms. That which stirs us transforms us—let those things you love do the same for all of your gracious spaces, inside and out.

A QUEEN'S ESCAPE

I am always taken by a grand house, and I have seen many: the seaside collection of mansion-size "cottages" in Newport, Rhode Island; the awe-inspiring Biltmore Estate in the foothills of Asheville, North Carolina; and one of my favorites, the magnificent Palace of Versailles in France.

At Versailles, I was struck by the centuries-old beauty that time had failed to diminish—the meticulously manicured gardens where a monarch might seek a moment of solace, the opulent residences of royals past, and the highlight of my visit, Marie Antoinette's arcadian escape, the Petit Trianon.

Ingeniously designed by Ange-Jacques Gabriel, the diminutive chateau was Marie Antoinette's undisturbed sanctuary, where the formal conventions of life at court bowed to the young Austrian queen's desire for simplicity, peace, and privacy.

Everything at Petit Trianon, from the lilac-scented groves to the abounding gardens to the elegantly decorated salons, was done *de par la Reine*, "by order of the Queen." Not even Marie

Antoinette's husband, King Louis XVI, was allowed to enter the sanctum without her say-so.

I was enchanted! I believe every woman deserves her own private oasis where *de par la Reine* is the ruling order. Women are God's caretakers; our husbands, children, and grandchildren and countless others in our lives depend on us to prepare meals, dole out heart and hospitality in equal measure, and attend to the minutiae of daily life. And, although most of us do so gladly, it is imperative that we take time each day to rejuvenate from the inside out with a space that inspires—whether it's a cascading waterfall with a quiet spot for reading or a cozy nook filled with those things that are familiar and well-loved.

I have built a career on this very belief; my magazines are testaments to that. Look at the pages of *Southern Lady*, *Victoria*, or *TeaTime*, and you will find each filled not only with recipes and entertaining ideas, but also with page after page of what we in the magazine industry refer to as "beauty shots."

How does this idea translate from magazines to the real world? By cultivating in our homes and havens a personal comfort zone that is "by order of the Queen." Go with whatever inspires you or sparks your interest—carve out a space where you can pursue an artistic passion, journal, or simply dawdle and daydream.

What I believe is most important, however, is a deliberate approach to carving out a "just-for-me space," which entails creating a sense of place with simple furnishings, personal touches, and, above all, an abundance of beauty to drink in.

UNEXPECTED BEAUTY

Finding the unexpected beauty in everyday things is one of my greatest pleasures. I have been known to spend hours arranging my closets just so—especially my shoes!—or plopping a plant or flower bouquet in a place where I might stumble upon it later and smile.

I have a dear friend who even takes the time to pretty up her pantry. Can you imagine? The rows of buttermilk paint-glossed shelves are all lined with mason jars, each filled with dry goods (plus a few marshmallows for midnight hot chocolate). Thrown into the mix are her collection of antique buttons, baskets of knitting materials, painting supplies, and a few framed pictures. She even installed a chandelier-style light fixture and a leaded-crystal door with panels of stained glass for added appeal.

I can't tell you how such devotion to creating beauty moves me—it's like giving yourself a little gift every day, a gift that nourishes the creative spirit that lives within us all.

STRIKE THE RIGHT NOTE

It is one thing to have a beautiful room, but it is another thing to have a room that excites you when you enter! I love being surrounded by gems and jewels that have been given to me by special people or that are souvenirs from my travels. And the more unusual the better; you can build an entire room around one item, from a lamp to a musical instrument.

Collections make a central decorating theme and, when used or displayed creatively, bring harmony and balance to a space or room. By incorporating your beloved collectibles, you not only enhance your design scheme but also have remembrances of antiquing afternoons and treasure hunts with friends.

PUT IT IN WRITING

Few things inspire me like the written word. Like any true Southern lady, I am well versed in and have a deep and abiding love for the art of personal correspondence. And make no mistake, in the times in which we live—a world of hurry-scurry e-mails and frantic text messages—a chatty letter from a friend or a thoughtful thank-you note from even the most casual acquaintance are items to treasure.

To inspire your own inner muse, create a dedicated space for the task. A beautiful writing desk, soft but sufficient lighting, and pen and paper are essential, but don't forget the intangible elements. A prettily framed collection of family photos, an antique quill and ink set, or an exquisite ink pen that simply feels good in your hands will unleash your inner voice—and that is the very essence of a gracious space.

{ ENCHANTING DETAILS }

*"Fashion is not something that exists in dresses only.
Fashion is in the sky, in the street, fashion has to do with
ideas, the way we live, what is happening."*

—COCO CHANEL, FASHION DESIGNER

The effortlessly elegant and endlessly quotable Coco Chanel once said of fashion: "Dress shabbily, and they remember the dress; dress impeccably, and they remember the woman." The same is true of a home. A truly gracious home is one that reflects the woman who lives there—from her hobbies and passions to her most cherished memories and loved ones. My home mirrors all of these things. In my kitchen and breakfast nook, there is china from my grandmother mixed in with mementos from my travels. Precious finds from antiquing sojourns with friends are tucked here and there throughout my guest parlor and great room, while romantic accessories and colors that replenish and rejuvenate me outfit my private living areas, such as the bedroom and bathroom.

In "Enchanting Details," we will concentrate on tapping into your inner muse to help fashion a home of serenity and splendor that reflects the woman within. At the end of each chapter, you will find journaling sections to help direct you in this quest. These are designed to combine practical elements of home design with personalized, inspired guideposts that will help you envision and create the home of your heart.

{ FEATHERING THE NEST }

Whether a stately castle or a humble cottage, your home should be a harbor not only for your body, but also your soul; a place that provides shelter and solace from the rest of the world. To create a restful dwelling, one that sustains body, mind, and spirit, you need not start from scratch. Start with what you have—and what you know.

GILDING THE LILY

Every home deserves a graciously appointed flower garden, and in the Southern states, where we bask in the sun for most months of the year, maintaining at least a patch or two of ornamentals is a joy to behold. I am particularly drawn to perennials; when they bloom anew year after year, it's like old friends coming back for a visit!

My preference is white flowers, but I love just about any color. Hydrangeas, the house flower of the South, always amaze me. Their gradient colors ascend from brilliant whites to blues to a shimmering antique green before their blooming season is over. At the height of hydrangea season, visitors will find their showy clusters blooming at my door and brightening the spaces of my home, inside and out.

And for me, the bloom is not off the rose even after it's been plucked. Pressing flowers is a centuries-old technique that flattens a blossom to a paper-thin texture. These can be framed, glued onto stationery to make a lovely greeting card, or pressed between glass frames and used as a tray. I have a wonderful hatbox that my mother covered with pressed flowers and then varnished.

Flower presses can be purchased, but one of the simplest techniques is to start with fresh flowers, then press the blossoms between the pages of a heavy book (using blotting paper to protect the pages) until thoroughly dry. Place a weighty object on the book—a brick will do—and leave it untouched for two weeks or so. The delicate results will bring you endless joy.

CUSTOMIZE YOUR SPACE

A dear friend who is an avid gardener recently searched and searched for the perfect new potter's bench, but couldn't find just what she wanted. Then inspiration struck. She used her old bench as the base and added a section of garden gate to the back for a pleasing new aesthetic. By modifying what she already had, my friend created something uniquely her own.

A trip to a local hardware store provided a bounty of tools specific to her gardening interests, and handles, hooks, and floral jugs to keep it all neatly organized. Now she not only has a functional workspace, but one that is attractive and perfectly customized to suit her tastes!

SCENT

"Stay me with flagons, comfort me with apples." I think of these words from the Songs of Solomon whenever I catch the faint fruited scent of ripened apples in the antique bowl that sits on my kitchen counter.

Scent is a powerful expression of soul-calming beauty, and you can enrich your home with fragrant purchased items or, even more fun, create a potpourri with what you have on hand.

The next time you bake an apple pie, freeze the peels and simmer them later with spices. The homey scent will enhance the ambience of your home and lift your spirits with every wafting whiff.

INVITING GUEST ROOMS

The art of hospitality wasn't invented by Southerners, but we certainly have perfected it! A guest room is a type of "home away from home" for visitors, and making people feel cared for is easy if you develop an eye for details.

Follow the advice of Emily Post and offer guests the best that you have. Don't skimp on furnishings, and bathe the room in a palette of cool, calming colors, preferably more neutral shades, with plenty of ambient lighting for added warmth. A guest room is a wonderful place to showcase unusual or antique fabrics—because they aren't frequently used and won't be subjected to so much wear and tear—as well as to display the overflow of your collections.

Little niceties will make your guests' stay a memorable one. Fill guest rooms with a generous abundance of bedside amenities, such as fresh flowers, a scented candle, and a carafe of spring water and tumblers for drinking. And don't neglect the necessities visitors will need for a comfortable stay, such as an alarm clock, a telephone in the room, extra hangers in the closet, and perhaps a television or radio. Stock the guest bathroom with petite bottles of hair-care and styling products, shower gels (for men and women), toiletry items, a hair dryer, and over-the-counter remedies to soothe temporary and minor ills.

And if your guest room features a beautiful view, make it a focal point; don't cover it up with curtains or shades. A restful spot for daydreaming is an integral part of welcoming shelter for visitors! Place a potted flower or plant on the windowsill to lead the eye to the garden or other vista beyond. Your guests will feel cool, calm, and collected with such beauty for respite.

A PERSONAL RETREAT

You may have heard the oft-told tale of how Anna, the Duchess of Bedford, "invented" afternoon tea in the nineteenth century. Seeking to stave off the "sinking feeling" that plagued her between meals, Queen Victoria's lady-in-waiting began secreting away each afternoon to her private chambers in Belvoir Castle to indulge in a spot of tea, finger sandwiches, and fresh pastries. Soon enough, members of her inner circle were invited to join her for the 4 o'clock ritual, and a social convention—one born of intimacy and friendship—was firmly established.

I have always adored this story; it speaks to me on every level as a woman. And it reminds me of the importance of a woman's bedroom. In the press of life and all its stresses, it is essential for every

woman to have a bedroom that is both a retreat and a sanctuary where she can rest, relax, and prepare herself to greet the day and welcome others (by invitation only) for secret-sharing and confidential conversations. It is a room that must serve many functions!

The first consideration is color. Our reactions to color are deeply personal, and in a bedroom, opt for tones that are tranquil to you. I am mad for red, but it is a hue that excites and energizes me. Blue, on the other hand, sets my eyes and spirit at ease, and it is the primary color in my bedroom, accented by honeyed neutrals that counter the coolness of blue with a touch of warmth.

The bed will doubtless serve as the primary focal point in your bedroom, so choose the best bedding you can afford in regally layered fabrics, as well as a beautiful headboard that adds to the feeling of luxury. Pull it all together with curtains, plump pillows, area rugs, low-lit lamps, and carefully chosen accessories that add to the atmosphere of serenity.

If you love needlework as I do, for instance, have a beautifully creweled remnant fashioned into a bed pillow, or use a length of crocheted swag as unique edging for your headboard. Be inventive!

{ FEAST FOR THE EYES }

Weddings, births, and betrothals, a simple celebration to mark the changing of the seasons—any occasion can be special if you make it so. From last-minute fancies to meticulously planned feasts, the time, care, and effort you put into sharing your home and hospitality with others will surely show in the details. And it is those seemingly inconsequential elements that people remember most, so stage the scene with care.

CALIFORNIA DREAMING

As a child, my favorite movie star was Lucille Ball. She wasn't just funny and beautiful; she epitomized glamour to me. In the fourth and fifth seasons, when the Ricardos and the Mertzes headed for Hollywood in search of fame and glory, I was thrilled.

I longed to follow in the footsteps of Lucy's madcap adventures; to run into William Holden (sans pie) in the Brown Derby or hatch a harebrained scheme to sneak into Cornel Wilde's penthouse. I too dreamed of holding court in Hollywood, shopping on Rodeo Drive, and spending endless summer days entertaining my friends beside my fabulous Olympic-size swimming pool.

To this day, a lush poolside vista says "California cool" to me—a touch of tropical flair combined

with comfortably casual chic that suits the season to a tee. And no matter where you live, a swimming pool (or any outdoor lounging area) can serve as your home's entertaining oasis during the sun-filled months of summer.

First, decide which elements will be permanent, such as statuary, overscaled planters, and other ornamental accounts; styles can range from nouveau neoclassical to Bahamian brio, so don't be afraid to mix and match motifs. Fill in with furnishings; all-season rattans and wickers are classic choices, but if you prefer wrought iron or weatherproof woods, that can work, too.

Overstuffed cushions in splashy island hues are fun, and no matter your price range, it's a great idea to purchase a set of china and serving pieces for poolside parties. Set a silver-screen-worthy poolside scene, and your summer will be filled with memorable moments!

PICNIC FOR ONE

I adore grandiosity—especially when it comes to creating lavish occasions. One of my favorite examples occurred in the summer of 1575, when Robert Dudley, the earl of Leicester, attempted to woo Queen Elizabeth I with an unheralded feast at his castle in Warwickshire.

Hoping to secure her hand in marriage, Dudley set the watermark for extravagance. The banquet lasted 17 days, during which the Queen and other guests wined and dined, danced, listened to a symphony, enjoyed masques, played chess, and were awed by after-dark fireworks displays.

The elaborate furnishings included banquet tables that groaned under the weight of the food, enormous silver bowls overflowing with fruit and grains, staged seating, bedding for reclining, carpets,

crimson satin curtains, columns, tapestries, and paintings. Dudley even commissioned a temporary 70-foot bridge that spanned the valley around his home, the castle at Kenilworth. Elizabeth turned down Dudley's proposal, but the three-week celebration became legendary and remains so to this day.

I love the romantic aspect of that fabled fete, and I think every woman deserves at least one such great party in her honor. If there is no randy young earl to throw it, you'll just have to contrive it for yourself.

In the summer, when the weather is balmy and beautiful, pack a picnic for one. This is a grand occasion for a special woman (you), so don't economize on the food—cook or buy gourmet goodies in servings for one, and don't skimp on the furnishings.

Even if it's no farther than your own backyard, pack a chair, a table, and linens to dress it, and ornate accents. And don't forget a restful activity—perhaps paints and canvas, a diary for journaling, or simply a good read. You will feel refreshed, relaxed, and ready to take on your world and all its challenges in no time. As I always say, treat yourself like a queen, and you will feel like one.

SOUTHERN TAPAS

The Spanish tradition of tapas is a favorite of mine, and I frequently co-opt this Castilian form of fellowship when I want to share special time with someone such as a dear friend or loved one.

In Spain, after-five crowds gather daily in special tapas taverns and fortify themselves with glasses of wine—traditionally sherry—and round after round of little bites of food. The appetizer-like repast can be hot or cold, elaborate as stuffed peppers and miniature sandwiches, or as simple as olives and cheese or skewered chunks of spicy fish or fowl. The lot is served on "little plates," in tidbit-size portions that are passed about, which serves to create by necessity a certain level of intimacy and conviviality.

Sound delightful? It is! And what a wonderful way to celebrate a special someone, perhaps a birthday or happy event, or even "just because." As atmosphere is such an important aspect of tapas, I try to create a unique sense of place by arranging my table for two in an unexpected area. In winter

months, that might be fireside or in my private study; when the weather turns warm, the patio or porch is an ideal spot, or even a roomy foyer for rainy days.

Set the table with care—opt for lovely but relatively simple linens, in colors that echo your surroundings, for a grounding effect. Avoid fussy centerpieces, which divert the focus from conversation and sharing, and concentrate instead on creating ambience. Glowing votives, a simple spray of flowers, and perhaps a pretty place setting will suffice.

Because I am Southern, I like to design a menu that speaks to the foodways with which I was raised, but I always try to amp up the elegance. Salmagundi, a colonial dish favored by the gentry of Virginia, might make an appearance at my tapas table, along with tiny pastry puffs stuffed with a Savannah cocktail of shrimp, artichoke, and cheese. And not only do I not skip dessert, I serve three courses—perhaps a bite-size confection or two followed by a showstopper, such as a flourless chocolate cake for two, drenched in ganache and garnished with fresh berries. Finding the perfect balance between good company, wonderful food, and a charmingly adorned space in which to serve it results in an unforgettable evening and a memory to treasure!

TIME WELL SPENT

If you are like me, you are lucky enough to have collected a group of dear women whose friendship has stood the test of time. These bonds of sisterhood enrich my life in so many ways, and I would be lost without that special circle of friends who know me better than I sometimes know myself.

One such friend, who owns a stunning seventeenth-century gaming table, puts this antique treasure to good use. Once a month or so, she bakes a batch of goodies and invites three mutual friends to join her for the afternoon. Together, they play chess or cribbage, Scrabble or bridge; whatever suits their fancy.

If you own such an exceptional piece, use it! If not, create your own "gaming" corner in a library or study. A four square table is the perfect size—not too many seats, nor too few—and a set of tapestried or antique chairs lends a layer of elegance. This dedicated recreational space will add a fun dimension to your décor and offer you a special place for spending time with others.

SUNSET FOR TWO

My two favorite times of day are early morning, when the mist hangs heavy and dew still clings to the roses that grow in my garden, and late afternoon, when the sun sinks into the sky, giving way to the dreaming moon.

Mornings are, by their very nature, solitary; in the peace and quiet, and under the spell of the sun's first rays of light, I think creatively and am able to calmly ponder the day to come as I sip my coffee or tea. By the end of the workday, however—after hours of business calls, meetings, and e-mails—I am often spent and in need of solace and comfort.

At such times, very little rejuvenates me like the setting sun. In waves of glowing color—drifts of arching pink and orange mingling with curls of yellow—the sun melts into the horizon. Such a spectacle of nature demands to be appreciated, and I am always a willing spectator; it's even more special when a like-minded companion joins me.

I love the idea of creating a "sunset theatre" to capture such pageantry. Pick a western facing spot, and outfit it with seating; comfort is absolutely key, so choose a comfy swing or glider, or perhaps a relaxing rocker, if that is more your taste. Add nothing more than a few colorful pillows and perhaps a lantern or two to light the path back, once night sets in.

A cooling concoction to drink, a few nibbles to sate your pre-dinner appetite, and a friend or loved one to share it with, and you're set for a truly spectacular show—one that will bring even the most hectic day to a close, suffused with beauty and simple joy.

{ FINISHING TOUCHES }

A bow on a present, the candles on a birthday cake, an intricate diamond clasp on a strand of pearls—these are unforgettable finishing touches, the little something extras that raise the bar from special to fabulous. The same applies in your home. With a thoughtful approach, you can create a wow factor in every room!

FEMININE FLOURISHES

Though our tastes and styles may differ, women tend to share a common appreciation for beauty and a keen attention to detail. Think of your favorite outfit. Every woman owns at least one ensemble that makes her feel on-top-of-the-world confident.

Maybe it's a suit that creates a stunning silhouette or a blouse in a shade that brings a certain color to your cheeks, but I'm willing to bet there is a never-fail choice hanging in your closet that you turn to when you need a little boost. I imagine you take care accessorizing that special outfit, too, from the perfect pair of pumps and matching handbag to a special shade of lipstick that makes you feel poised and cool—no detail is overlooked.

Now, think of your home with the same sense of aesthetics. If you take the time to dress yourself carefully, shouldn't you expend just as much care and effort in your dwelling? Your home doesn't have to be just a place you live, eat, and sleep—it can also be a true sanctuary, one that

uplifts and soothes. Achieving this means mastering a few basics, then embellishing with details that add an unmistakable layer of polish.

To my mind, a feminine room is not necessarily one draped in baby-soft pastels and chintzy florals, but rather it is a space that carries an obvious "woman's touch." At Monticello, I was incredibly fascinated by Thomas Jefferson's constant attempts to capture the beauty of nature inside and out, but I was also struck by the absence of feminine flourishes in the widower's Virginia estate.

A woman can leave a mark on a room in the smallest ways. If you are a romantic, look for soft colors not only in the bigger pieces—such as a chair or a bed—but also in the accessories. Try using (or handcrafting if you have the skill) soft pillows and throws, winsome window treatments, frilly

patterned rugs, and froufrou tabletop items. If you are drawn to East-Coast classic, opt for more neutral tones in a blue, brown, or gray palette and brighten with punches of color. For this style, choose fewer but exquisitely detailed accessories that draw the eye and arouse interest, perhaps a sterling silver comb and brush set for your vanity or antique boxes and bowls filled with unique keepsakes, such as Champagne and wine bottle corks.

Don't be afraid to try anything new with accessory pieces—items of interest, objects of art, throw rugs, pillows, table lamps, baskets, candleholders—the options are endless. If the idea doesn't work, you can always undo or update it. The more permanent choices—furniture, wall color, floor coverings, and architectural features—tend to cost more in time and money to replace, so be more thoughtful in these selections. But the finishing details are easily refurbished and highly expressive, so have fun with them!

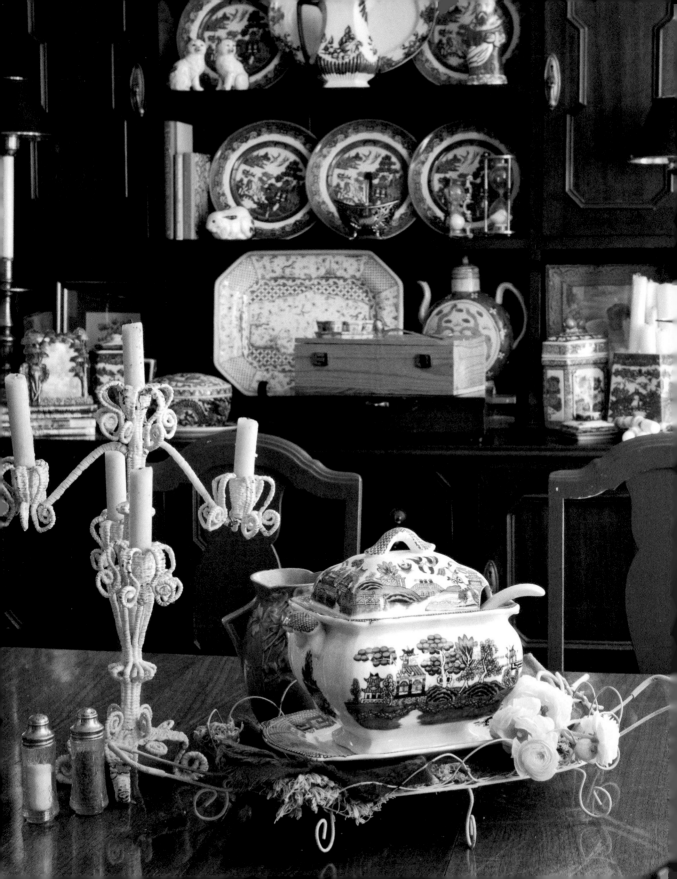

COLORFUL ACCENTS

My love affair with blue and white began decades ago and has never wavered. The combination of delft blue and snowflake white still excites me! This deceptively simple combination of colors is calming, yet very stimulating to my creativity. I love finding new ways to bring refreshing ideas to rooms using blue and white in fabrics, in china, and in accent pieces throughout my home.

One trick I love is pairing these special pieces with colors that make them pop. Vibrant sunshine yellow is a favorite, because it fairly snaps and crackles against the deep blue and crisp white and creates such a cheerful palette for any room. Tiny touches of a zesty orange have the same mood-lightening effect. Take the bright yellows or oranges away and add white or ivory instead, and the mood is more serene.

You can do the same with any color scheme of your choosing. Emphasize dual-tone designs with a third hue that plays to the strengths of your chosen color companions.

Chocolate and pink, sea blue or seedling green with earthy brown, ultra-vibrant shades with pure white—all are color schemes that have enjoyed enormous popularity in the last few years. Throw a third shade or a distinctive repeating pattern such as toile into the mix and you bring depth, balance, and interest to the look. Walnut and sage will harmonize perfectly with coral or violet, for instance, while on the other end of the style spectrum, yellow and white will pair handsomely with cherry red or hunter green. Be daring in your color choices. Again, finishing touches aren't necessarily meant to last forever, so be bold and don't worry too much about matching shades.

The key is to use the third tone sparingly enough to avoid a "busy" look but evenly enough to achieve balance and scale. You can keep a room or space fresh by alternating undertones with the season (or your mood for that matter). Even subtle variations can make a huge impact!

CUT FLOWERS

Like a little black dress that fits the bill for every occasion, flowers are always your best and most perfect accessories—they are not only pleasing to the eye but also stress-relieving. And mind you, this is not only my opinion; it is a proven scientific fact!

A behavioral study recently conducted by Harvard Medical School and Massachusetts General Hospital tested a group of 54 people in the 25-to-60 age range using flowers as a daily part of home décor. Half of the participants in the flower wellness study were given home décor

accents other than flowers, and the other 50 percent lived with flowers on a daily basis for a week. The findings came as no surprise to me. The group given flowers to enjoy reported feeling more energetic and more optimistic after looking at them, especially first thing in the morning.

What's more, those same people consistently reported feelings of well-being that lasted through the day. So despite their limited shelf life, flowers don't provide just instant gratification. Flowers offer lasting joy! They enrich our homes and lift our spirits—whether it's a sweet and simple nosegay at a place setting, an artfully intricate arrangement in the living room, or a few stem poking out of a bud vase or bottle perched in a windowsill.

Flowers offer an endless array of color, texture, shape, and fragrance—there is literally a perfect bloom for everyone!

If you have the time, talent, and inclination, growing your own decorative flowers is a wonderful idea. Not only does a cutting garden enhance the outdoor landscape, it also affords you the added stress-reducing benefit of nurturing flowers as they grow.

To ensure a steady supply of material for building bouquets, cultivate a mix of long-stemmed annuals, perennials, herbs, and foliage-bearing plants. Your best bet is a typically sunny spot with good drainage laid out in beds with roomy rows. Because these flowers will be regularly snipped, don't worry too much about the ornamental elements of design. Instead, concentrate on maintaining a mix of enthusiastic bloomers and stagger growth patterns so that something pretty is always in production.

And don't forget those herbs, which provide a hint of fragrance and greenery to floral arrangements as well as a constant source of culinary options for the kitchen. Snip, wash, and add fresh herbs to savories and sweets; use them to create lovely gifts (perfect for flavored vinegars and oils); or simply secure herbs in bundles and hang them upside down to dry for later use in cooking.

{ ARTFUL EMBELLISHMENTS }

"A person with real flair is a gambler at heart."

—BILLY BALDWIN, INTERIOR DESIGNER

Just as every wardrobe requires a seasonal update, every home benefits from the occasional "space lift." Not necessarily a complete overhaul, mind you—although that can be fun, too—but more of a "freshening." Even subtle twists and changes can absolutely transform a space. Don't believe me? Place a bouquet of flowers in a room, and your eye will go to it every time you enter. Why? Because women are both creatures of detail and fans of the familiar. That's what makes us so interesting!

In "Artful Embellishments," I will share some of my favorite tips, tricks, and techniques to help you overcome design obstacles, envision new ways of looking at old spaces, and make the most of what you already have on hand. We will mix and match his-and-her spaces, learn to capitalize on our collections, and much more. And remember, these are only suggestions; in fact, I encourage you to take my ideas and find inventive, ingenious new ways to make them your own. In the words of the venerable Billy Baldwin: "Be faithful to your own taste, because nothing you really like is ever out of style."

{ IMPARTING ELEGANCE }

Elegance, like anything else, is in the eye of the beholder. Like a diamond with many facets, true gentility expresses itself in a diverse range of styles and tastes. I think the late designer Yves Saint Laurent summed up the subject very well when he said: "Never confuse elegance with snobbery." Whether you are a person who prefers a cozy "shabby chic" look or someone who opts for more urbane sophistication, a stylish home is easily attainable with a little know-how and confidence!

SHEER BEAUTY

I have always loved floor-to-ceiling windows, which Madame de Rambouillet said "make a room extremely cheerful and permit one to enjoy, without hindrance, the air, the view, and the pleasure of the garden." The words of this seventeenth-century French society maven still ring true today, and this style of window remains a wonderful way to enlarge a space or enhance a room with high ceilings.

When a space features such a strong architectural element, why not accentuate it? A window treatment of sheer drapery panels affords a bit of privacy, while still letting in natural light. A chair or table with simple lines and perhaps a pretty pillow that echoes the pattern of the draperies make a statement without making a fuss. The fluid fabric adds a touch of classic style, but subtly so. The understated accents allow the real star of the space to shine through!

CREATIVE DISPLAYS

As most of the people who know me well can tell you, when I first discovered Colonial Williamsburg, I also discovered creamware. My collection has been growing exponentially ever since. The thought of purchasing these precious pieces and then shutting them away in a dark cabinet or pantry to collect dust pains me, so I constantly challenge myself to find new ways to display them. I want to really live with what I love, not just own it.

I urge you to do the same. Plates can be just as pretty on the wall as on the table, and a glass bell jar intended for a garden can be stunning as the cloche cover for a pedestaled dessert. Think outside the box, and you will be amazed at the possibilities you can envision!

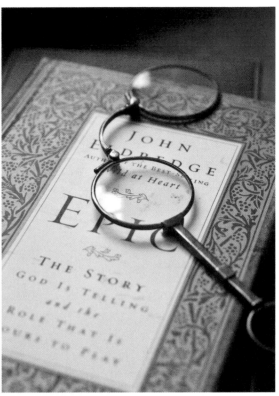

NATURE'S CHARM

I have a friend who owns the most beautiful antique secretary. Situated next to a picture window overlooking her gardens and paired with a comfy velvet-covered chair, the desk is her favorite daydreaming spot. It is there that she not only pens all her personal correspondence, but also feels relaxed enough to sip a cup of tea and thumb through a magazine, read a book, or simply gaze at the pink and yellow roses blossoming in the sun just outside the window and in the bud vases that adorn her desk. Even her drapes mirror the flowers growing within view!

Elements that mimic the outdoors—especially the scenery within view—bring natural and timeless beauty, whatever your taste or style. It's difficult to improve upon God's mastery and incorporating the motifs of nature makes for a setting that is effortlessly elegant and innately calming. To achieve the look and create your own indoor oasis, choose accents in nature-friendly colors and patterns, such as a floral window treatment, and soften with seasonal flowers or greenery.

BALANCING ACT

Finding the right balance in a room brings not only beauty, but harmony. Factors to consider include color, texture, mass, and number. Light hues enlarge a room, so it only makes sense that choosing wall colors and furniture in pale shades will increase the visual scope. Fill in with darker tones in small doses—this works particularly well when using patterned fabrics and accent pieces. If you want to make a larger room seem cozier, go the opposite direction with darker walls and light colors for trims, moldings, ceiling, furniture, and accessories.

Apply the same sense of proportion when choosing furnishings. Opt for a balanced mix of sizes and shapes in the pieces you select—counter a boxy sofa with a round or oval coffee table, for instance—and match weighty pieces with smaller ones. When accessorizing, think in numbers. The eye tends to

love odd numbers, so try wall groupings and tabletop displays in groups of three, five, and seven. It is an old insider secret employed by floral artists and stylists; the next time you see a bouquet or arrangement that really wows you, focus in on the repetition of particular blossoms. You will undoubtedly discover that different flowers show up in odd numbers. The same techniques will work in your favorite rooms.

And although it's a little trickier to define, don't forget the emotional balance of a room or space. Walk through your home and make note of your reactions to each room. Do you feel peaceful, energized, soothed, relaxed, or (heaven forbid) tense? Now, concentrate on what is conjuring those feelings—is it your color choices; does the room feel too crowded or overly sparse? Is there ample seating? Does it reflect your personality? Once you've answered those questions, focus on the areas that need changing and think of ways to warm up the space. Oftentimes, you'll find the fix is as easy as adding a pillow or two, an area rug, or even a few scented candles!

Swatch Palette

Creating a gracious space involves mixing and matching patterns in your fabrics and furnishings—trust your instincts and have fun with it!

1. What types of fabrics and patterns are you drawn to in your personal wardrobe? How can you creatively weave those same styles into your design schemes?

_____

_____

_____

_____

_____

_____

_____

2. Are there common motifs or fabrics you are drawn to, such as toile, florals, or stripes? How can you build on that within a given space?

_____

_____

_____

_____

_____

_____

_____

_____

3. Describe the feel or mood that exists within a room or space. What patterns or designs come to mind?

_____

_____

_____

_____

_____

_____

_____

4. Select a favorite object or collectible and build around it. What patterns visually jibe with it—
florals, stripes, solids, or others?

_____

_____

_____

_____

_____

_____

_____

_____

{ TREASURED KEEPSAKES }

I think people too often make the mistake of confusing value with cost. A keepsake may indeed be a priceless antique or piece of art. But it can also be as simple and sweet as an enamelware coffeepot, given to you by a friend, that now serves double duty as a lovely container for garden blooms. Finding unique ways to display and use the treasures you've collected will add to the joy of owning them.

LOVELY LIGHT-CATCHERS

Although it's not what I have chosen for my own home, I think the vintage cottage look that has become so popular in recent years is absolutely adorable. This kitschy style is a precious blend of nostalgia, romantic charm, and eclectic elements.

A dear friend who was "cottage" before it was popular has created a sanctuary all her own using an impressive collection of off-the-wall items that reflect her interests and personality. One of her favorites is a lovely collection of vintage soda-pop bottles displayed in her sunny kitchen. She uses these flea-market treasures any time she has a few stems from the garden that need a container and places them on a windowsill, where they catch the sunlight like a prism. She has cleverly added a few stoppered crystal and inexpensive glass bottles, pieces from cruet sets, decanters, wine bottles, and even a few old-fashioned Mason jars. The overall effect is irresistibly charming!

VARIATIONS ON A THEME

You will inevitably find that growing one collection leads to adopting another. For me, my love of teacups has, over time, inspired additional collections, including teapots, linens, and accoutrements such as silver strainers and hand-carved wooden tea caddies.

Whatever you enjoy acquiring, I suggest developing a relationship with a neighborhood antiques dealer. Drop in their store often and ask questions. These learned people will help steer you in the direction of undiscovered collectibles, educate you on the value and provenance of pieces, and let you know when interesting newcomers arrive that might add a wonderful new dimension to your collection!

HIS & HERS

Not every woman is in love with soft pastel shades—which is just fine. On the other end of the color spectrum is an array of more neutral hues from which to choose. From creamy bisque to deep chocolate brown to punchy mustard yellow, these golden shades envelop a room in a natural incandescence that holds the light and bathes every surface in a subtle but unmistakable glow. The added benefit is that these colors are also gender-neutral and lend themselves beautifully to mixing his-and-her styles in any room.

Believe me, I understand that mixing and matching your beautiful keepsakes and his treasured belongings can be a challenge. But it can be done, and finding the perfect balance often begins with

choosing a gender-friendly color scheme. Underpin the palette with neutral colors in warm or cool tones, then embroider with softer feminine shades—lemony yellow, minty green, shimmering blue, or a subtle cranberry.

Try the same his-and-her approach with furniture. In a sitting or living area, for instance, a brass lamp with simple lines and a gender-neutral clock or plant will offset an ornate brocade chair and ottoman. To unify the space without tipping the scales as either too "hers" or too "his," blend your mutual collections into a balanced whole. You might hang your antique transferware plates alongside his European roe deer antlers (trust me, he'll love you for it). Or display his golfing trophies with your set of silver julep cups.

And do consider that although you need your space, he needs his, too. Rooms with a dedicated function, such as a library or study, can carry a more heavy-handed masculine design scheme. Here, opt for somber tones and virile textures—supple leather, gleaming wood, and bronze or iron furnishings. Then fine-tune with framed photos, figurals, and fabric elements that enhance the personality of the space.

BOOK SMART

If asked, I would be hard-pressed to pinpoint my favorite book, but among my perennial favorites are *The Notebook*, by Nicholas Sparks; the classic *Little Women*, by Louisa May Alcott; and anything from the Mitford series, by the lovely Jan Karon.

You will find these and many other titles lining the bookshelves of my home and office. But with their graphic and colorful covers, books can lend an intriguing nuance to a decorating scheme when used as accessories. Leather-bound collections impart an especially elegant note to almost any space.

Use a variegated stack as a platform for votive holders, or display books in sets using unique bottom-heavy accessories, such as snow globes or garden statuary, as bookends. I've even seen stacks of books used as the base for a glass-topped coffee table. Just make sure the books are balanced in size and that the spines are facing outward, so that guests can read them. It's not only charming, but a conversation-starter, too!

THE WRITE TOUCH

In the South, we learn as children to write personal letters and thank-you notes. The written word is an important aspect of the etiquette of famed Southern hospitality because a hand-scripted line or two never fails to let the recipients know they are cared for and appreciated.

A beautifully appointed journaling desk makes the task so much more pleasurable, so create a writing space that inspires you! You'll need an organized, well-lit area, a holder for letters and desk accessories, and a dictionary for reference. Don't forget the extra touches that will help encourage chatty correspondence, such as a fragrant bouquet of flowers, personal photos, and a lamp for softly diffused lighting.

Also, consider investing in a really luxurious ink pen and the best wardrobe of stationery (paper, thank-you cards, and blank note cards) you can afford; cotton paperstock is particularly recommended. It will make writing and mailing your letters and notes an unparalleled pleasure.

Color Palette

{ COOL }

{ EARTHY }

{ SERENE }

{ ROMANTIC }

Color Journal

Choosing a color palette can prove a difficult task—a few inspirational questions will help you get started.

1. Consider your favorite flowers—tulips, buttercups, zinnias, hydrangeas, Gerbera daisies, or roses. How can you use those colors to create a soothing sanctuary in your home?

_____

_____

_____

_____

_____

_____

_____

2. What is your favorite season? How can the color palette that signifies that season be incorporated into your decorating scheme?

_____

_____

_____

_____

_____

_____

_____

_____

Color Palette

{ COASTAL }

{ SPICY }

{ TROPICAL }

{ ELEGANT }

Color Journal

3. Name an era of fashion that strongly appeals to you—timeless Chanel, the mod sixties, or perhaps the glam-filled forties, and the colors that were popular then. How can those styles and colors be used to attire your spaces?

_____

_____

_____

_____

_____

_____

_____

_____

4. Choose something that belongs to someone you love—perhaps a piece of jewelry from your mother, or your father's favorite silk tie. How can you use those colors in a way that creates a gracious space and reminds you of your loved one every time you see it?

_____

_____

_____

_____

_____

_____

_____

_____

{ NOOKS & CRANNIES }

When you were a little girl, did you ever make a "secret clubhouse" with your sister or friends? I did. Using my mom's dining-room chairs as support and her bedsheets as "walls," we transformed my family's den into a private escape where we shared more secrets, giggles, MoonPies, and hot chocolate than I care to remember! These days, my sister and I have replaced those living-room forts with adult-size sanctuaries and creative spaces. With a little space and a lot of ingenuity, you can do the same.

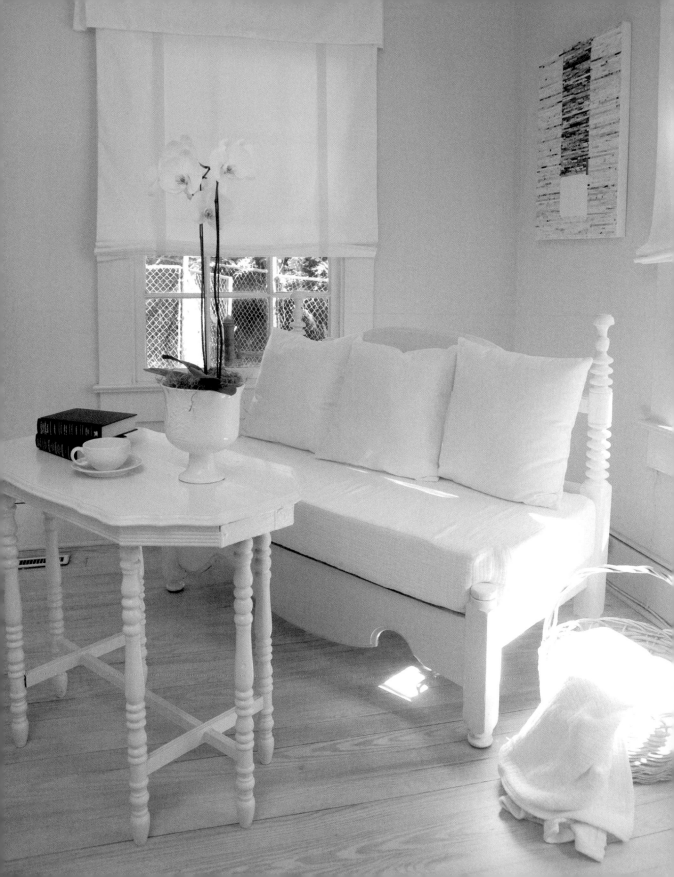

SENTIMENTAL VALUE

I have a dear friend who, as an empty nester, suffered the pangs of missing her college-age daughter. Clever, creative lady that she is, however, she found a wonderful way to remember her daughter at home, while dealing with the fact that she was away at school.

She hired a craftsman to reconfigure her daughter's childhood bed into a darling settee, which she used as the anchor of a cozy sanctuary nook in a sunny room. Now, when my friend wants to take a little time out for herself, she has a special place all her own—one that reminds her of her precious daughter. Giving a little face lift to a piece of furniture with sentimental value is a fantastic way to bridge the gap between old and new and create a one-of-a-kind personal refuge!

PANTRY SPACES

From the "butt'ries" of Colonial American homes to turn-of-the-century Hoosier cabinets, our love affair with pantries is well established, and rightfully so. Equal parts storage and workspace, and typically located between the kitchen and dining rooms, a butler's pantry can be an indispensable home feature.

Once hidden out of sight behind closed doors, however, the modern butler's pantry is making a stylish return. It's a masterfully multifunctional space that can be used as a staging area for entertaining and for displaying fine tablewares when not in use.

To dress it up, add a few accessories, such as a lamp for subtle lighting, a piece of art or two, or open shelving for additional storage and display. A wine cooler, small fridge, or sink can also prove helpful—particularly during dinner parties, special occasions, or milestone events!

UPSTAIRS, DOWNSTAIRS

Although they're popular spots for displaying holiday decorations, Christmas greenery, and seasonal accessories, high-traffic stairwells and landings are often considered "wasted spaces" and are woefully underestimated as areas that can carry visual impact.

For tighter quarters, a seating-for-one area can be a lovely focal point—especially when situated near a pretty window. It will be filled with plenty of natural light during daylight hours, and naturally draw attention to an eye-catching window treatment. Floor or table lamps can be added for the shift to evening. For a low-lit subtle glow, try sconces or even wall-mounted candleholders instead.

And don't forget the space at the foot of the stairs. Curving and split-level staircases form a natural enclosure at the base that begs to be brightened up and filled! It's a perfect spot for an antique sideboard or table, showy chairs, and art. Much like a hallway or foyer, this transitional space eases the eye from one part of the house to the next, so take a look at the surrounding rooms when choosing color schemes, décor styles, and furnishings.

The stairs need flair too and not just at Christmas. The wall space is perfect for displaying original art, prints, and treasured photographs of loved ones. Hang framed pieces at eye level or above, preferably grouped in odd numbers to create a more dramatic focal point. Looping swags or garlands using seasonal greenery, fabric, or ribbons enliven the banister, while newels offer an inviting perch or spot for candles, flowers, or whatever strikes your fancy and suits the space.

Motifs Journal

Crown molding, trims, and columns can add polish to a room, so pick the elements and accents that best reflect your personal style.

1. What rooms or elements of a room (such as a fireplace, door casing, or stairs) might most benefit from crown moldings, columns, or trims?

_____

_____

_____

_____

_____

_____

_____

2. What hardware in the room, such as drawer pulls or door fixtures, will either compete with or complement your chosen millwork?

_____

_____

_____

_____

_____

_____

_____

Decorative Motifs

Motifs Journal

3. Inventory the rooms of your home and the mood you would like each one to convey. What style of medallion, decorative trim, or other motif might best enhance the feel of each room?

_____

_____

_____

_____

_____

_____

_____

4. What periods of architecture or even history are you most drawn to? What motifs were popular during that period and how can you adapt these subtle motifs to your own style?

_____

_____

_____

_____

_____

_____

_____

_____

{ RECIPES }

Foods to Prepare and Share

In the South, we list our recipes among our most precious and prized keepsakes and heirlooms. Whether it's a discovery from a church cookbook, a favorite magazine, or a hand-me-down from our mothers and grandmothers, we treasure our favorite recipes almost as much as our silver!

Southerners also believe in sharing a good thing. Here, you will find a few of my personal favorites—each menu item is found in the pages of the book, and each one is suited to any number of special occasions!

{ THE SOUTHERN LADY AT HOME }

Apple Streusel Coffee Cake
Makes 10 to 12 servings

1 ½ cups finely chopped Granny Smith apples
½ cup raisins
½ cup chopped pecans
½ cup firmly packed brown sugar, divided
¾ teaspoon ground cinnamon, divided
½ cup butter, softened
½ cup sugar
¾ cup sour cream
2 large eggs
2 teaspoons vanilla extract
1 ½ cups all-purpose flour
1 teaspoon baking powder
½ teaspoon baking soda
¼ teaspoon salt
¼ cup toffee bits
½ cup confectioners' sugar
2 to 3 teaspoons milk

Preheat oven to 350°. Grease and flour a 9-inch round cake pan. In a small bowl, combine apple, raisins, pecans, ¼ cup brown sugar, and ½ teaspoon cinnamon; set aside. In a medium bowl, combine butter, sugar, and ¼ cup brown sugar. Beat at medium speed until creamy. Add sour cream, eggs, and vanilla, beating until well combined. In a small bowl, combine flour, baking powder, baking soda, and salt. Gradually add flour mixture to butter mixture, beating until well combined. Spread half of batter in prepared pan; sprinkle apple mixture over batter. Spread remaining batter over apple mixture; sprinkle with toffee bits. Bake for 45 to 50 minutes, or until a wooden pick inserted in center comes out clean. Cool for 10 minutes; remove from pan and cool completely. In a small bowl, combine confectioners' sugar, ¼ teaspoon cinnamon, and 2 teaspoons milk. Add additional milk if thinner consistency is desired. Drizzle over cooled cake.

Strawberry Patch Cake
Makes 1 triple-layer cake

1 cup butter
1 ¾ cups sugar
5 egg whites
2 teaspoons strawberry extract
2 cups pureed strawberries
½ cup sour cream
3 cups cake flour
1 tablespoon baking powder
1 teaspoon baking soda
¼ teaspoon salt
1 recipe Southern Strawberry Icing
  (recipe follows)
Garnish: fresh strawberries

Preheat oven to 350°. Grease and flour 3 (9-inch) cake pans. In a large bowl, beat butter and sugar at medium speed with an electric mixer until fluffy. Beat in egg whites, one at a time, beating well after each addition. Stir in strawberry extract, pureed strawberries, and sour cream. Sift together cake flour, baking powder, baking soda, and salt. Gradually add to butter mixture, beating until combined. Pour batter evenly into prepared pans, and bake 28 to 30 minutes, or until a wooden pick inserted in center comes out clean. Let cool in pans 10 minutes. Remove from pans and cool completely on a wire rack. Spread Southern Strawberry Icing between layers and on top and sides of cake. Garnish with fresh strawberries, if desired.

Southern Strawberry Icing
Makes 3 ½ cups

¼ cup butter
1 (8-ounce) package cream cheese, softened
¼ cup pureed fresh strawberries
½ teaspoon strawberry extract
6 ½ cups confectioners' sugar

In a large bowl, beat butter and cream cheese with an electric mixer at medium speed until smooth. Add pureed strawberries and strawberry extract, beating until combined. Gradually beat in confectioners' sugar until smooth.

Tip

177

Both of these recipes call for sour cream, which adds flavor and almost always ensures a moist crumb in baked goods. Other add-ins that will help remedy dry cake layers include pudding mix, cream cheese, and even a quarter-cup or so of mayonnaise! These work especially well with commercial cake mixes.

{ AFTERNOON TEA }

Poppy Seed Chicken Salad in Phyllo Cups
Makes 30 phyllo cups

2 cups chopped cooked chicken
1/2 cup finely chopped apple
3 tablespoons minced celery
2 green onions, minced
1/4 cup sour cream
1/4 cup mayonnaise
1 teaspoon lemon juice
1 teaspoon honey
1 teaspoon poppy seed
1/4 teaspoon salt
1/4 teaspoon ground black pepper
2 (2.1-ounce) packages frozen phyllo cups, thawed
Garnish: chopped fresh chives

In a medium bowl, combine chicken, apple, celery, and green onion. In a separate bowl, combine sour cream, mayonnaise, lemon juice, honey, poppy seed, salt, and pepper. Combine sour cream mixture with chicken mixture. Spoon into phyllo cups. Garnish with chives, if desired.

Spicy Pecan Pimiento Cheese Sandwiches
Makes 4 cups pimiento cheese

2 cups grated sharp Cheddar cheese
1 cup grated Monterey Jack cheese
1 cup grated Pepper Jack cheese
1 cup mayonnaise
1/2 cup diced pimientos
1/4 teaspoon ground black pepper
1/2 cup finely chopped Spicy Pecans

(recipe follows)
8 slices wheat bread, crusts removed
Garnish: pimento cheese, pecan half, parsley

In a medium bowl, combine cheeses, mayonnaise, pimientos, and pepper. Using an electric mixer at medium speed, beat until creamy. Cover and chill. Stir in Spicy Pecans. Spread pimiento cheese evenly on 4 bread slices; top with remaining bread slices. Cut each into fingers. Garnish with one-half teaspoon of pimento cheese, pecan half, and parsley, if desired.

Spicy Pecans
Makes 2 cups

2 tablespoons butter, melted
2 teaspoons hot pepper sauce
1 teaspoon chili powder
1/2 teaspoon garlic salt
1/4 teaspoon cayenne pepper
2 cups pecan halves

Preheat oven to 200°. Line a baking sheet with aluminum foil. In a small bowl, combine butter, pepper sauce, chili powder, garlic salt, and cayenne pepper. Add pecan halves, tossing gently to coat. Spread pecans in a single layer on prepared baking sheet. Bake for 30 minutes. Remove from oven and cool completely.

Ham and Apricot Pinwheels
Makes 24 pinwheels

1 (8-ounce) package cream cheese, softened
1/4 cup finely chopped dried apricots

2 tablespoons apricot preserves
3 large flour tortillas
12 thin slices deli ham
Garnish: apricot preserves, chopped fresh
  parsley

In a small bowl, combine cream cheese, dried apricots, and apricot preserves. Spread one-third cream cheese mixture onto each flour tortilla. Place four slices of ham on top of cream cheese mixture. Roll up tortillas, wrap tightly in plastic wrap. Chill 1 hour, and cut into spirals. Garnish with apricot preserves and parsley, if desired.

Tip

The spicy pecans that give my favorite pimiento cheese (often called the paté of the South) such a delicious kick are just as delicious on their own! Add them to salads, toss them in a savory snack mix, or keep them around as an anytime treat. Stored in a tin or pretty jar, they also make wonderfully charming hostess or holiday gifts!

{ AFTERNOON TEA }

White Chocolate Macadamia Nut Drop Scones
Makes 20 scones

2 cups all-purpose flour
1/3 cup plus 2 tablespoons sugar, divided
1 1/2 teaspoons baking powder
1 teaspoon baking soda
1/2 teaspoon salt
6 tablespoons unsalted butter, cut into pieces
1/2 cup white chocolate chips
1/2 cup chopped macadamia nuts
2/3 cup buttermilk
1 large egg, lightly beaten
1 teaspoon vanilla extract

Preheat oven to 350°. Line 2 baking sheets with parchment paper. In a large bowl, combine flour, 1/3 cup sugar, baking powder, baking soda, and salt. Using a pastry blender, cut in butter until mixture resembles coarse crumbs. Add white chocolate chips and macadamia nuts; mix well. In a separate bowl, whisk together buttermilk, egg, and vanilla extract. Add buttermilk mixture to flour mixture, stirring until dough is just combined. Drop by heaping teaspoonfuls onto prepared baking sheets; sprinkle with remaining sugar. Bake for 14 to 16 minutes, or until lightly browned.

Ooey Gooey Bars
Makes 24 bars

1 (18.25-ounce) package yellow cake mix
1/2 cup butter, melted
3 large eggs, divided

1 (8-ounce) package cream cheese, softened
4 cups confectioners' sugar
1 cup peanut butter baking chips
1 cup toffee bits, divided
Garnish: sifted confectioners' sugar

Preheat oven to 350°. Spray a 13x9x2-inch baking pan with non-stick cooking spray with flour. In a medium bowl and using an electric mixer at medium speed, beat cake mix, butter, and 1 egg until combined. Press mixture into bottom of prepared pan. In a medium bowl and using an electric mixer at medium speed, beat cream cheese until fluffy. Add 2 eggs and sugar; beat until well combined. Fold in peanut butter chips and 1/2 cup toffee bits. Pour cream cheese mixture over cake mix mixture in pan. Sprinkle remaining toffee bits on top. Bake for 45 minutes. Garnish with confectioners' sugar, if desired.

Lemon Mexican Wedding Cookies
Makes about 36 cookies

1 cup unsalted butter, softened
1/3 cup confectioners' sugar
1 tablespoon lemon zest
1/2 teaspoon lemon extract
1/2 teaspoon vanilla extract
2 1/4 cups all-purpose flour
1/4 teaspoon salt
Confectioners' sugar
Garnish: fresh lemon zest

In a medium bowl, combine butter and 1/3 cup confectioners' sugar. Using an electric mixer at medium speed, beat until fluffy (approximately

2 minutes). Add lemon zest, lemon extract, and vanilla extract, beating until combined. Add flour and salt, beating to combine well. Cover and chill for 1 hour. Preheat oven to 350°. Line 2 baking sheets with parchment paper. Roll chilled dough into 1-inch balls. Place 1 inch apart on prepared baking sheets. Bake for 15 minutes, until set, but not browned. Cool 5 minutes. Roll in confectioners' sugar. After cookies have cooled completely, roll in confectioners' sugar a second time. Garnish with lemon zest if desired.

Tip

Scones are lovely any time of day, but they are an absolute must at teatime. If white chocolate or macadamia nuts don't suit your palate, don't be afraid to experiment with different flavors. Try butterscotch or chocolate chips, almonds, hazelnuts, or pecans. Dried fruits also work, or other flavors, such as ginger or citrus zest!

{ TIME WELL SPENT }

White Chocolate Coffee
Makes 5 cups

4 ounces white chocolate, chopped
2 ½ cups whole milk
2 ½ cups freshly brewed coffee
Garnish: whipped cream and white
　　chocolate curls

In a medium saucepan over medium-low heat, combine white chocolate and milk. Heat until steaming, but do not boil. Whisk until white chocolate is melted and smooth. Stir in coffee. If desired, garnish with whipped cream and white chocolate curls. Serve immediately.

Chocolate Chip Cranberry Cookies
Makes about 4 dozen

1 cup unsalted butter, softened
1 ¼ cups firmly packed brown sugar
½ cup sugar
2 large eggs
1 teaspoon vanilla extract
2 ¼ cups all-purpose flour
1 cup quick-cooking oats
1 teaspoon baking soda
½ teaspoon salt
1 cup sweetened dried cranberries
1 (12-ounce) package semisweet chocolate
　　morsels

Preheat oven to 350°. Lightly grease a baking sheet. In a large bowl, beat butter, brown sugar, and sugar with an electric mixer until fluffy. Beat in eggs and vanilla. In a medium bowl, combine flour, oats, baking soda, and salt. Gradually add to sugar mixture, beating until combined. Stir in dried cranberries and chocolate morsels. Drop mixture by tablespoons onto prepared baking sheet. Bake 12 to 14 minutes, or until golden brown. Cool for 2 minutes on baking sheet. Remove to wire racks to cool completely.

Peanut Butter Chocolate Chip Cookies
Makes about 4 ½ dozen

½ cup unsalted butter, softened
½ cup crunchy peanut butter
½ cup firmly packed brown sugar
½ cup sugar
2 large eggs
1 ¾ cups all-purpose flour
1 teaspoon baking soda
¼ teaspoon salt
1 (4-ounce) bar semisweet chocolate, melted
1 cup chopped salted peanuts

Preheat oven to 350°. Lightly grease a baking sheet. In a large bowl, combine butter, peanut butter, brown sugar, and sugar. Beat with an electric mixer until creamy. Beat in eggs. In a small bowl combine the flour, baking soda, and salt. Gradually add to peanut butter mixture, mixing well. Roll dough into 1-inch balls, and place on prepared baking sheet. Bake for 10 to 12 minutes, or until edges are lightly browned. Cool on wire racks. Drizzle with melted chocolate, and sprinkle with chopped peanuts.

Georgia Toffee
Makes about 3 dozen pieces

13 graham cracker sheets
1 cup unsalted butter
1 cup firmly packed brown sugar
1 (14-ounce) can sweetened condensed milk
1 cup semisweet chocolate morsels
1 cup chopped pecans

Preheat oven to 425°. Line a 10x15-inch jellyroll pan with heavy-duty aluminum foil. Spray foil with nonstick cooking spray. Place graham cracker sheets evenly over foil, breaking crackers apart as necessary to evenly cover bottom of pan; set aside. In a medium saucepan, combine butter and brown sugar. Bring to a boil over medium-high heat; boil for 2 minutes. Remove from heat; stir in condensed milk. Immediately pour evenly over crackers. Sprinkle evenly with chocolate morsels and pecans. Bake for 12 minutes. Let cool. Cut into diamond shapes, if desired.

Tip

Even those who don't bake frequently enjoy making cookies, and one of the bonuses is they can be made months in advance for later use. Almost all cookie dough freezes beautifully—just be sure each batch is tightly sealed in a double layer of plastic wrap. Pre-baked cookies can be frozen also; pack them in layers of waxed paper and thaw in a low-heat oven (300° or so) for a few minutes before serving.

{ SUNSET FOR TWO }

Blue Cheese Deviled Eggs
Makes 1 dozen

2 tablespoons olive oil
1/8 ounce prosciutto, chopped
1/2 teaspoon minced garlic
6 large eggs, hard-boiled and peeled
1/4 cup mayonnaise
2 tablespoons crumbled blue cheese
1/2 teaspoon Dijon mustard
1/8 teaspoon ground white pepper

In a small skillet, heat olive oil over medium heat. Add prosciutto and garlic; cook for 5 minutes, stirring constantly. Remove from heat; set aside to cool. Halve eggs lengthwise. Remove yolks, and place in a small bowl. Mash yolks with a fork, and stir in mayonnaise, blue cheese, mustard, white pepper, and prosciutto mixture until well combined. Fill egg whites evenly with yolk mixture.

Lemon and Prosciutto Stuffed Mushrooms
Makes about 3 dozen mushrooms

3 (8-ounce) packages fresh baby bella
   mushrooms, wiped clean
2 tablespoons butter
1 (5-ounce) package prosciutto, chopped
1/3 cup minced fresh chives
2 (8-ounce) packages cream cheese, softened
2 tablespoons Dijon mustard
1 tablespoon fresh lemon zest
1 teaspoon dried tarragon
1/2 teaspoon ground black pepper

Preheat oven to 350°. Remove stems from mushrooms. Finely chop enough mushroom stems to equal 1/3 cup. Discard remaining mushroom stems. In a large skillet, melt butter over medium heat. Add prosciutto, chives, and chopped mushroom stems. Cook, stirring frequently, for 6 minutes, or until prosciutto is crisp and mushrooms are tender. Reduce heat to low. Add cream cheese, mustard, lemon zest, tarragon, and pepper, stirring until mixture is combined. Remove from heat. Spoon cream cheese mixture evenly into mushroom caps; place on a rimmed baking sheet. Bake for 20 minutes. Serve immediately.
Note: Mushrooms can be stuffed 2 days ahead. Cover, and refrigerate. Bake before serving.

Margarita Shrimp Cocktail
Makes about 18 servings

60 fresh jumbo shrimp, unpeeled
1/2 cup tequila
1/4 cup olive oil
1/3 cup chopped fresh cilantro
3 tablespoons fresh lime juice
1 teaspoon salt
5 cloves garlic, minced
Prepared cocktail sauce
Garnish: chopped fresh cilantro

Peel shrimp, leaving tails intact; devein, if desired. In a large stockpot, bring 10 quarts of water to a boil. Add shrimp, and boil 3 to 5 minutes, or until shrimp are pink. Drain well; rinse with water; set aside. In a large bowl, combine tequila, olive oil, cilantro, lime juice, salt, and garlic. Add shrimp, cover, and chill 1 hour. Drain shrimp, discarding marinade. Serve with prepared cocktail sauce. Garnish with chopped fresh cilantro, if desired.

Raspberry Lemonade Punch
Makes about 1 gallon

8 cups water
¾ cup lemonade-flavor drink mix
1 (12-ounce) jar prepared raspberry syrup
1 (12-ounce) can frozen pink lemonade
   concentrate, thawed
1 (2-liter) bottle cold ginger ale

Combine water, drink mix, syrup, and pink lemonade concentrate, whisking to combine; refrigerate. Before serving, add ginger ale and serve immediately.

Cranberry Spritzer
Makes about 5 quarts

1 (46-ounce) can pineapple juice
1 (32-ounce) bottle cranberry juice
1 (12-ounce) can frozen lemonade
   concentrate, thawed
1 (2-liter) bottle ginger ale, chilled
Garnish: frozen cranberries

In a large pitcher, combine pineapple juice, cranberry juice, and frozen lemonade concentrate. Chill until ready to serve. Before serving, slowly add ginger ale and stir gently to combine. Garnish with frozen cranberries, if desired.

Tip

I always try to have the makings for a few good appetizers on hand, just in case company drops in. Versatile cream cheese, great for sweet and savory items, is an ideal staple, as are flavorful cheeses, such as Brie or manchego. A selection of condiments (pesto sauces, chutneys, mustards, etc.) adds instant flavor, and ready-made bases, such as crackers and frozen pastry shells, make easy work of pulling together a last-minute spread in a snap.

{ PICNIC FOR ONE }

Artichoke and Asparagus Pasta Salad
Makes 2 servings

1 cup penne pasta, uncooked
1 cup asparagus, sliced on the diagonal into
   1-inch pieces
¼ cup shredded Parmesan
2 tablespoons fresh minced parsley
1 lemon, zested and juiced
2 tablespoons olive oil
½ teaspoon salt
½ teaspoon freshly ground black pepper
1 (6-ounce) jar marinated artichoke hearts

Bring water to a boil in a medium stockpot. Add penne and cook for 6 minutes. Add asparagus to water and cook for 1 minute. Drain and place in an ice-water bath. In a small bowl, whisk together the lemon zest, lemon juice, olive oil, salt, and pepper. Add artichoke hearts, lemon juice mixture, Parmesan, and parsley. Drain pasta and asparagus. Add to artichoke mixture, tossing gently to combine.

Chicken Salad with Pecan Dressing
Makes 2 servings

1 chicken breast, cooked and shredded
½ cup sliced red grapes
½ cup sliced Granny Smith apple, cut into
   1-inch pieces
1 tablespoon Dijon mustard
2 tablespoons minced shallot
2 tablespoons honey
2 tablespoons white balsamic vinegar
2 tablespoons extra virgin olive oil
½ teaspoon salt

½ teaspoon freshly ground black pepper
¼ cup toasted pecans, chopped

In a medium bowl, combine chicken, grapes, and apple. In a small bowl, whisk together mustard, shallot, honey, and balsamic vinegar. Slowly pour in olive oil, whisking to incorporate. Add salt and pepper, and whisk to combine. Stir in pecans. Pour dressing over chicken mixture, tossing gently to combine. Serve immediately.

Spinach Salad with Avocado Dressing
Makes 1 serving

2 cups loosely packed fresh spinach
¼ cup thinly sliced red bell pepper
¼ cup black-eyed peas, drained and rinsed
¼ cup sliced hearts of palm
¼ cup Avocado Dressing (recipe follows)

In a small bowl, toss together spinach, red bell pepper, black-eyed peas, and hearts of palm. Drizzle with Avocado Dressing.

Avocado Dressing
Makes 4 servings

1 large avocado
1 garlic clove
¼ cup extra virgin olive oil
3 tablespoons lemon juice
2 tablespoons mayonnaise
½ teaspoon salt
½ teaspoon freshly ground black pepper
In the bowl of a food processor, puree avocado

with garlic clove. Add olive oil while running to help smooth. Add lemon juice, mayonnaise, salt, and pepper. Pulse until well blended; refrigerate until ready to serve.

Note: Refrigerate unused dressing in an airtight container for up to 2 days.

Minted Fruit Salad
Makes 2 servings

1 tablespoon honey
½ lemon, juiced
1 orange, zested and segmented, juice
    reserved
1 tablespoon minced fresh mint
⅓ cup 1-inch cubed honeydew
⅓ cup 1-inch cubed cantaloupe
⅓ cup 1-inch cubed pineapple

In a small bowl, whisk together honey, lemon juice, orange juice, orange zest, and mint. Add honeydew, cantaloupe, and pineapple, tossing gently to combine.

Lemon Mint Spritzer
Makes 1 serving

2 tablespoons lemon juice
2 tablespoons sugar
3 cups sparkling water
8 to 10 mint leaves
1 lemon, thinly sliced
Cucumber slices (optional)

Combine lemon juice and sugar in a microwave-safe container. Microwave on HIGH in 30-second intervals until sugar dissolves; cool. Pour lemon syrup into a serving carafe. Add sparkling water, stirring to combine. Add mint leaves, lemon slices, and cucumber slices. Serve over ice, if desired.

Tip

187

I adore picnics; they appeal to the part of my nature that wants to make a grand celebration of even the simplest moment. I find that adding lavish little extras makes the occasion even more special. For instance, hand linens slightly doused in a bit of lemon-laced water and stored in a plastic bag provide easy, elegant clean-up after the meal. Or try offering guests sprigs of freshly parsley or mint—both are natural breath fresheners.

{ SOUTHERN TAPAS }

Cheese Puffs with Shrimp and Artichoke Filling
Makes 6 servings

½ cup water
¼ cup butter
½ cup all-purpose flour
¼ teaspoon salt
2 large eggs
½ cup finely grated Gruyére cheese
1 recipe Shrimp and Artichoke Filling
  (recipe follows)
Garnish: fresh chives

Preheat oven to 400°. Line a baking sheet with parchment paper. In a small saucepan, bring water and butter to a boil over medium heat. Using a wooden spoon, beat in flour and salt, stirring constantly, until mixture forms a ball. Remove pan from heat, and let cool for 5 minutes. Add eggs, one at a time; beat with a wooden spoon for 30 seconds after each addition, until smooth. Add cheese, stirring until smooth. Spoon or pipe mixture into 6 equal mounds, 2 inches apart, on prepared baking sheet. Bake for 30 to 35 minutes, until golden and puffy; cool on wire rack. Cut off top ⅓ of each pastry; remove and discard soft dough inside. Spoon Shrimp and Artichoke Filling into bottoms of cheese puffs. Garnish with fresh chives, if desired.

Shrimp and Artichoke Filling
Makes 6 servings

2 tablespoons olive oil
3 tablespoons finely chopped green onion
3 tablespoons finely chopped red bell pepper
1 teaspoon minced garlic
⅓ cup finely chopped baby bella mushrooms
⅓ cup finely chopped artichoke hearts
2 tablespoons dry white wine
½ pound medium fresh shrimp, peeled,
  deveined, and coarsely chopped
1 (3-ounce) package cream cheese, softened
⅓ cup freshly grated Parmesan cheese
1 teaspoon Dijon mustard
¼ teaspoon salt
⅛ teaspoon ground black pepper
⅛ teaspoon ground red pepper

In a medium sauté pan, heat olive oil over medium-high heat. Add green onion, bell pepper, and garlic; cook for 2 minutes, stirring constantly. Add mushrooms, artichoke hearts, and wine; cook for 3 minutes. Add shrimp; cook for 3 minutes, or until pink and firm. Reduce heat to medium-low. Add cream cheese, Parmesan cheese, Dijon mustard, salt, black pepper, and red pepper. Stir until cheese is melted.

Boursin and Prosciutto Stuffed New Potatoes
Makes 1 ½ dozen potatoes

9 small new potatoes
1 (5.2-ounce) package garlic and herb-
  flavored Boursin cheese
½ cup chopped prosciutto
¼ cup sour cream
2 teaspoons chopped fresh parsley
¼ teaspoon salt
¼ teaspoon ground black pepper

Preheat oven to 400°. Line a baking sheet with

aluminum foil; set aside. Place potatoes in a large saucepan, in enough water to cover, and boil until fork tender, about 8 to 10 minutes. Drain, and let cool. Cut potatoes in half crosswise; cut a thin slice off round end of each potato to stabilize on a serving plate. Using a melon baller, scoop out centers of potatoes, leaving a ¼-inch-thick shell. Place potato pulp into a medium bowl. Add cheese, prosciutto, sour cream, parsley, salt, and pepper. Mash with a potato masher until well combined. Spoon mixture evenly into potato shells. Place on prepared baking sheet, and bake for 18 to 20 minutes, until lightly browned. Serve immediately.

Salmagundi Croustades
Makes 1 ½ dozen croustades

¼ cup mayonnaise
½ teaspoon Dijon mustard
1 tablespoon chopped fresh tarragon leaves
¼ teaspoon ground black pepper, divided
¼ cup vegetable oil
1 tablespoon white wine vinegar
⅛ teaspoon salt
18 toasted French bread rounds
1 ½ cups finely shredded green leaf lettuce
1 cup finely chopped smoked turkey
4 hard-boiled eggs, sliced
¼ cup finely chopped red onion

In a small bowl, combine mayonnaise, Dijon mustard, tarragon, and 1/8 teaspoon pepper; set aside. In a separate bowl, combine oil, white wine vinegar, salt, and remaining ⅛ teaspoon pepper. To assemble, spread a thin layer of mayonnaise mixture on each toasted French bread round. Layer with lettuce, smoked turkey, sliced egg, and red onion. Drizzle with vinaigrette mixture. Serve immediately.

Tip

A favorite pastime of mine is reading historic cookbooks. I'm always interested in learning how women generations before me lived, and I find such pleasure in thinking of inventive new ways to carry forward the traditions of our collective past. These Salmagundi Croustades, for instance, were born of my love of colonial history. I took the basic elements of the popular seventeenth-century salad of meats, egg, and vegetables dressed in vinaigrette and created a bite-size savory that is elegant and delicious.

Flourless Chocolate Cake for Two
Makes 1 (6-inch) cake

½ cup semisweet chocolate morsels
6 tablespoons butter
3 large eggs, separated
1 teaspoon vanilla extract
½ cup sugar
1 tablespoon unsweetened cocoa powder
⅛ teaspoon salt
½ cup hot fudge topping
Garnish: chocolate curls, fresh raspberries

Preheat oven to 325°. Fill an 8x8-inch pan with 1 inch of hot water, and place in oven. Spray a 6-inch round cake pan with baking spray and line bottom with parchment paper; set aside. In a small microwave-safe bowl, melt chocolate and butter on HIGH (100 percent power) for 30-second intervals, stirring after each, until melted and smooth (approximately 1½ minutes total). Cool chocolate mixture slightly. In a medium bowl, whisk together egg yolks and vanilla until well combined. Whisk in chocolate mixture until smooth. In a separate bowl, combine sugar, cocoa, and salt. Stir sugar mixture into chocolate mixture until well combined. In a separate bowl, beat egg whites with an electric mixer at medium speed until soft peaks form. Fold egg whites into chocolate mixture in thirds. Spoon batter into prepared pan. Place in oven, in center of square pan. Bake for 50 to 55 minutes, or until a wooden toothpick inserted in center comes out clean. Remove cake from water bath; cool in pan on wire rack 10 minutes; remove from pan and cool completely. To serve, heat hot fudge topping according to package directions; spoon over top of cake. Garnish with chocolate curls and fresh raspberries, if desired.

Cherry Almond Truffles
Makes about 1 dozen

1 (8-ounce) package cream cheese, softened
¼ cup confectioners' sugar
½ cup slivered almonds, finely chopped
½ cup finely chopped red candied cherries
½ teaspoon cherry extract or almond extract
1 (11-ounce) package white chocolate morsels
1 tablespoon shortening
Garnish: sliced almonds

Line a baking sheet with parchment paper; set aside. In a medium bowl, combine cream cheese and confectioners' sugar. Beat at medium speed with an electric mixer until creamy. Add almonds, cherries, and cherry extract, beating to combine. Cover and chill for 2 hours. Roll cream cheese mixture into 1-inch balls, and place on prepared baking sheet. Freeze for 4 hours to overnight. In a medium microwave-safe bowl, melt white chocolate and shortening on HIGH for 30-second intervals, stirring after each, until melted and smooth (approximately 1½ minutes total). Using wooden toothpicks, dip each ball into candy coating. Garnish tops with sliced almonds, if desired.

Sugar Cookie Cups with Strawberry Clotted Cream
Makes 1 dozen

½ (16.5-ounce) package refrigerated sugar cookie dough
4 ounces cream cheese, softened
¼ cup sour cream
1 tablespoon strawberry extract
¼ teaspoon vanilla extract
¼ cup heavy whipping cream
6 tablespoons confectioners' sugar

Garnish: fresh strawberries, pink sugar, fresh mint

Preheat oven to 350°. Roll cookie dough into 1-inch balls. Press into bottom and halfway up sides of one (12-cup) mini cheesecake pan. Bake for 12 minutes; remove from oven. In pan, gently press inside of baked cookie dough to form cups. In a medium bowl, combine cream cheese, sour cream, strawberry extract, and vanilla extract. Beat at medium speed with an electric mixer until smooth. In a separate bowl, beat cream at high speed with an electric mixer until soft peaks form. Add confectioners' sugar and beat until stiff peaks form. Fold whipped cream mixture into cream cheese mixture. Cover and chill. To serve, spoon or pipe strawberry cream mixture into cookie cups. Garnish with fresh strawberries, pink sugar, and fresh mint, if desired.

Tip

When it comes to cooking, "easy does it" is a golden rule for me. Sugar Cookie Cups with Strawberry Clotted Cream is about as simple as it comes; commercial cookie dough takes most of the work out of baking, while upping the ante on presentation. Apricot, peach, lemon, or raspberry filling would be a sweet substitute. You can also try pairing other prepared doughs with complementary fillings. Peanut butter, oatmeal, or chocolate chip dough would be divine teamed with vanilla, chocolate, or butterscotch fillings.

{ ACKNOWLEDGMENTS }

{ COVER }
The home of Brad and Robin Kidd was used for the cover shot, as well as the images on pages 46, 47, 48, 49, 50, and 51. We thank them for their generosity!

{ PAGES 38-43, 72- 73 }
The work of Adrienne Alldredge, stylist for *Southern Lady*, appears in the sections "Expressions in Color" on pages 38-43 and "Feathering the Nest" on pages 72-73.

{ PAGES 160-163 }
The styled settings that appear on pages 160-163 were part of the 2007 Birmingham Decorators' Show-House, sponsored by the Symphony Volunteer Council for the Alabama Symphonic Association, inc.

Student designers from the School of Interior Design, Virginia College at Birmingham were: Debbie Coleman, Margaret DiNella, Emily Glass, Emily Kelso, Courtney Panneton, Laura Panneton, Kina Ruggs, Courtney Spencer, Jami White, and Amy Wood.

Class Instructor Deborah Hastings managed the project, as well as the student designers in their efforts. Many heartfelt thanks!